The Berlin Blues

The Berlin Blues

Drew Hayden Taylor

Talonbooks

Talonbooks
278 East 1st Avenue, Vancouver, British Columbia, Canada V5T 1A6
www.talonbooks.com

Fifth printing: March 2014

Typeset in New Baskerville
Printed and bound in Canada on 100% post-consumer recycled paper

Cover design by Adam Swica

Talonbooks gratefully acknowledges the financial support of the Canada Council for the Arts, the Government of Canada through the Canada Book Fund, and the Province of British Columbia through the British Columbia Arts Council and the Book Publishing Tax Credit.

Library and Archives Canada Cataloguing in Publication

Taylor, Drew Hayden, 1962–
      The Berlin blues / Drew Hayden Taylor.

A play.
ISBN 978-0-88922-581-7

      I. Title.

PS8589.A885B47 2007   C812'.54   C2007-907144-9

Acknowledgements

As with any theatre production, a lot went into the creation and development of this play. First of all, thanks to Lighthouse Theatre Festival in Port Dover, Ontario. I did the first workshop of the play there one cold and snowy day.

Perhaps the biggest thanks should go to Native Voices, run by the dynamic duo of Randy Reinholz and Jean Bruce Scott, the petri dish for a lot of the native theatre that is being developed in the United States. They and their committed staff brought this baby to term.

And I suppose I should thank all the German people out there who have a special place in their hearts for Winnitou and all other native related things. This is my special homage to you.

A special thank you to my mother, to Janine, to Chris Reher, to my community and to just about anybody else that has ever read anything I've written. Sorry if I've left you out but whose fault is that?

Drew Hayden Taylor

The Native Voices at the Autry world premiere of *The Berlin Blues* by Drew Hayden Taylor (Ojibway) was produced March 1–25, 2007 at Autry National Center/Wells Fargo Theater in Los Angeles with the following cast and crew:

ANDREW	Gil Birmingham
ANGIE	DeLanna Studi
TRAILER	Robert Vestal
DONALDA	Adeye Sahran
BIRGIT	Ellen Dostal
REINHART	Michael Matthys

Directed by Randy Reinholz (Choctaw)
Executive Producers: Jean Bruce Scott
and Randy Reinholz
Lighting Design: R. Craig Wolf
Scenic Design: Susan Scharpf
Costume Design: Christina Wright
Sound Design: Janna R. Lopez Raven
(Taos Pueblo, Yaqui)
Dramaturg: Oliver Mayer
Musical Director: Alex Wright
Choreographer: M. Isabel Schleeter
Dialect/Accent Coach: Paul St. Peter
Production Stage Manager: Dale Alan Cooke
Technical Direction: Nate Getrich
Assistant Director: Ian Skorodin (Choctaw)
Assistant Lighting Designer: Ashley Johnstone
Master Electrician: Leigh Allen

ACT ONE

Scene One

A small office used by the Reserve Police. OFFICER ANDREW is on the phone, lazily tossing darts at a dart board. ANGIE enters quietly, obviously in love with him.

ANDREW

(*on phone*) No. I'm sorry but you're wrong. I don't care what you saw on *Crime Stoppers*. James Benojee did not rob that bank in Oshawa last month. I know it for a fact. (*Pause.*) Well, for one thing, he wouldn't know where Oshawa is. Secondly, he's sixty-eight years old. And finally, he's in a wheelchair. (*Pause.*) I don't care if they're both bald. Baldness is not a crime. (*Pause.*) No I will not go over and put a scare into him anyways. I know you two have a dispute over road access but try to leave the police department out of this. Okay? Fine. Bye, Mom. (*Hangs up the phone.*) Jeez! Only thirty more thrill-packed years to go 'til retirement.

ANGIE

I love you.

ANDREW

If I had a nickel for every woman that's ever said that to me …

ANGIE

You'd probably have to borrow money.

ANDREW
> Angie, let me take you away. Let's run off to the Caribbean, right now. We'll drown our sorrows in rum and sand.

ANGIE
> And leave all this?

ANDREW
> Somehow I think this Reserve and the universe will survive without me doing the paperwork.

ANGIE
> As sweet as the Caribbean sounds, I'll have to pass. It's that job thing. Denise down at the arts and crafts store wants me to work an extra hour for the next two weeks. I've been told to do a quick inventory and set up a new sweetgrass and dreamcatcher display in a further attempt to exploit and demean our sacred and ancient culture by cynically capitalizing on its spirituality and uniqueness. But I'm not bitter.

ANDREW
> You hide it well. Why so busy?

ANGIE
> Seems some important people are coming to town. Germans, I think. Remember the last time a busload of Germans came through, they bought the place out. Denise even sold them her dog, claiming it was a breed unique to the Ojibway people.

ANDREW
> I remember that dog. It was a German Shepherd.

ANGIE
> I rest my case. Denise and Gary will pawn anything off as authentically Native. Here, I brought you a present.

ANDREW
> Buckskin scented shampoo. Why do you work at the store if it upsets you so much?

ANGIE

Hey, a girl's gotta do something to survive. I just have to balance my righteous indignation with a compulsive need to eat. Usually reality makes hypocrites of us all.

ANDREW

You know, most tourist shops don't employ ethical martyrs.

ANGIE

Well, we like to be different. Also, I do plan to go to the Caribbean with you, my sweetie, and that takes another fine gift the White man gave us. It's called money, of which far too much of mine goes to a wealthy White man named Tim Horton.

ANDREW

Anyway, I take it you're here for a reason?

ANGIE

I am. Your mother ...

ANDREW

My mother? I was just talking to her. What's she up to now?

ANGIE

Well, she would like us ...

ANDREW

... would like us to do what ...?

ANGIE

... to come for dinner.

ANDREW

Dinner!? That's it? No volunteer painting of the bingo hall? No donating ten percent of our salary to the Church? No having grandchildren by the weekend. Just dinner?

ANGIE

Just dinner.

ANDREW

It sounds like a trap.

ANGIE
You're awfully suspicious. For a cop.

ANDREW
We're taught to profile, and I've been profiling my mother for twenty-five years. I know what to expect. You should see the mental file I have on her.

ANGIE
Andrew, she's not a criminal.

ANDREW
Oh, you don't know the pain and anguish she's caused. On numerous instances she has broken into and entered my room without permission. Assaulted my person on several occasions with a large and lethal wooden spoon. She has forcibly confined me to my room …

ANGIE
I think that one's called being grounded.

ANDREW
Are you taking her side?

ANGIE
I love your mother.

ANDREW
It's all part of her master plan. Why didn't she mention dinner to me just now?

ANGIE
Probably because she knew you'd act like this. You two have the most peculiar relationship. I told her "yes" for dinner. What time do you get off work tonight?

ANDREW
The usual. I just have to go visit Trailer and have a chat.

ANGIE
Ah yes, Trailer. Say hello for me. Where are you meeting him?

ANDREW
At his trailer.

ANGIE
Ah yes, Trailer and his funny little trailer.

ANDREW

The last time I was over there it was like his lights were on but nobody was home.

ANGIE

Trailer?

ANDREW

No. His trailer. The Band council has been talking about doing something about Trailer and his trailer for a long time. Just a big fat brown thing that just sits there. Kinda embarrassing.

ANGIE

Trailer?

ANDREW

No. His trailer. Some people say that bolt of lightning that hit last summer may have caused some damage.

ANGIE

To the trailer?

ANDREW

No, to Trailer.

ANGIE

I'm going back to work now.

Scene Two

DONALDA KOKOKO's economic development office at the Band Administration building. It is deserted. Then suddenly, TRAILER sticks his head in. TRAILER, in his thirties, is a man of little ambition and even littler means. But he is content with his lifestyle.

TRAILER
Pretty Gal? Hello.

There is no response and he decides to enter. He picks up one of the books on her desk and opens it.

TRAILER
Twenty-first Century Aboriginal Economic Viability Paradigms. Hmm, that sounds like treaty talk. I always say never trust any words with more than three syllables in them.

He puts the book down and sits in a chair. Waiting. Bored, he finally goes to DONALDA's desk and uses the phone.

TRAILER
(*in a fake voice*) Yes please. Hi. My name is ... John Dunbar, and I have a meeting with Donalda Kokoko. I'm in her office but she doesn't seem to be ... (*Pause.*) Thank you very much.

Satisfied, he hangs the phone up and sits back down again. Then over the loudspeaker:

ANNOUNCEMENT/INTERCOM
Donalda, you have somebody waiting in your office. Thank you.

A few seconds later, DONALDA rushes into her office, with a cup of coffee splashing around..

DONALDA
I'm sorry, I wasn't expecting you so soon ...

She spots TRAILER and stops rushing immediately.

DONALDA
Trailer, what do you want?

12

TRAILER
    Hi Pretty Gal.

DONALDA
    Don't call me that. You know perfectly well my name is
    Donalda.

TRAILER
    But I've always called you Pretty Gal. Every since you were
    a pretty little gal. Everybody calls you that.

DONALDA
    Not anymore. I haven't been an *gal* in an awfully long
    time. If you want to talk to me, call me by my given name.

TRAILER
    Okay. Donalda.

DONALDA
    What do you want, Trailer?

TRAILER
    Your love.

DONALDA
    I'm economic development. Delusions are one office over.
    Right next to Welfare. Go away. I have a meeting.

TRAILER
    I cleaned my trailer.

DONALDA
    Don't care. Do you want a job? I can help you with a job.

TRAILER
    Making you happy would be my full time job.

DONALDA
    Let's see, the Hell Freezing Over office is downstairs in
    the Land Claims Settlement department. Trailer, I'm not
    interested. Why do you keep doing this? Embarrassing
    yourself and me. It's been over fifteen years goddamnit!

TRAILER
    Not to me.

DONALDA

We only went out for three months. Three friggin' months, fifteen years ago! Trailer, I've had colds that lasted longer than that.

TRAILER

It was like yesterday.

DONALDA

I've had two kids since then. Can't do that since yesterday.

TRAILER

I'd call them mine. Really, I would. They could stay in the back room of the trailer.

DONALDA

That's where your hot water tank is.

TRAILER

Warmest place in the trailer. See! I care.

DONALDA

Jesus, Trailer. There's more to life than that stupid thing. You've lived in that trailer your whole life. So did your parents. So did your grandparents. Your family has lived in that thing so long, pretty soon a bunch of anthropologists will be digging up your back yard.

TRAILER

That trailer is a family heirloom. I refuse to feel embarrassed due to a family tradition.

DONALDA

That's why people call you Trailer. Your real name is Fabian. That's a beautiful name.

TRAILER

So is Pretty Gal. I just want you to know I still care.

DONALDA

That's sweet. Sad but sweet. Trailer, Let me say this for the last time. You live in a fifty-year-old trailer. You wear the same clothes you had in high school. You don't have a job ...

TRAILER

I have a job.

DONALDA

You play bass in a country rock band. On Thursdays, Fridays, and Saturdays. That's not a job. It's a hobby.

TRAILER

It's not a hobby. It's a career. If you'd come and hear me, maybe ...

DONALDA

Trailer. I don't have time for this. You do this practically every month and it's gotta stop.

TRAILER

I just want you to know I'm persistent. That's kinda endearing ... isn't it? Charming, maybe? I can be very appealing when I want.

DONALDA

Jesus Trailer, your underwear is showing.

TRAILER

(*puzzled*) Underwear?

> *Suddenly, there's a knock at the door and two people appear. A smartly-dressed man and woman, both with briefcases stand at DONALDA's door. They speak with obvious German accents.*

BIRGIT

Excuse me. We are seventeen minutes early but we are looking for Ms Donalda Kokoko.

DONALDA

Of course, of course. The Germans. I'm Donalda Kokoko. Welcome to Otter Lake.

BIRGIT

Thank you. Or meegwetch, I believe, is the local linguistic response.

TRAILER

Di ... what?

BIRGIT

I am Birgit Heinze and this is Reinhart Reinholz.

REINHART

I bring greetings from the Teutonic people.

DONALDA
> Welcome to Otter Lake.

TRAILER
> I'm sorry. What was your name again?

BIRGIT.
> Birgit Heinze.

TRAILER
> Beer gut?!

BIRGIT
> Birgit.

TRAILER
> Beer gut ... and I thought we had weird nicknames.

BIRGIT
> I'm sorry, but you are ...?

TRAILER
> Oh yeah, uh I'm Trailer Noah.

BIRGIT
> Trailer ... hmn, is your name indicative of your Aboriginal heritage? Possibly because you are such a good tracker and trailer of deer and other such animals? That is why you are called Trailer?

TRAILER
> Yeah. That's me.

DONALDA
> Mr. Noah was just leaving. Goodbye, Mr. Noah. Co-obmen.

BIRGIT/REINHART
> Ah, co-obmen.

BIRGIT
> English translation: I'll be seeing you later.

REINHART
> Because there is no word in Ojibway for goodbye. Or for hell.

BIRGIT
> Or for tomato. Excellent. Please continue.

TRAILER
> Really! I didn't know that. (*to DONALDA*) Did you know that?

DONALDA
> Like I said. Mr. Noah was just leaving.

TRAILER
> Will I see you tonight? Tomorrow night?

DONALDA
> Only if I die today and you come to my wake.

TRAILER
> But Pretty Gal …

DONALDA
> Shut up. Go.

> *She strongly ushers TRAILER out of her office.*

BIRGIT
> Interesting gentleman.

DONALDA
> Only if you're a psychiatrist. You two have come a long way to visit our little community. To what do we owe this pleasure?

BIRGIT
> Yes, well, to business then. Mr. Reinholz and I are here to meet with you, your Chief and your council. We are business partners with a company called—

> *DONALDA reads their business cards.*

DONALDA
> —German Recreational Entertainment, Arts & Technology.

BIRGIT
> Affectionately known as GREAT. We believe we have developed what will be a fabulous enterprise for the people of Otter Lake. One that could change everybody's life, for the better.

DONALDA
> You got my attention.

BIRGIT
Yes, you see, there is a *great* interest in our country for Native People. It goes back a hundred years or so to a writer named Karl May who wrote many adventure novels about North American indigenous people.

REINHART
We think there is a unique opportunity to capitalize on that interest.

DONALDA
How? Vacation packages? Bus tours? Sweet grass flavoured beer? That kind of stuff?

REINHART
Think bigger. Think huger.

DONALDA
Bigger? Huger? What exactly are you guys getting at?

BIRGIT opens her briefcase and takes out some plans that she lays across DONALDA's table.

DONALDA
What are these?

BIRGIT
Plans, Ms Kokoko. Plans for the future, and plans for success. More specifically, plans for a Native theme park designed by Mr. Reinholz. We want to call it, are you ready, OjibwayWorld! Are you not amazed?!

DONALDA
Did you say—OjibwayWorld?

REINHART
Yes we realize you as a people prefer to be called Anishnaabe but for marketing purposes, it was decided to go with the more internationally known name of Ojibway. Regardless, OjibwayWorld will be the biggest and best in the world.

DONALDA
The biggest and the best! There are others?! Wait a minute ... I don't understand. You want to build a theme park, with rides and games and stuff like that, about the

Ojibway … That … that's a new one on me. I see here
where you have the bumper canoes.

BIRGIT

And over here we have the Medicine Ferris Wheel. Here's
the Four Directions shuttle service to get everybody
around. Turtle Island Aquarium. Whiskeyjack Pub and
Bar. The hotel will be called the Haida-Way. Get it?
Haida-Way? We've researched this quite extensively.

DONALDA

OjibwayWorld. Well, I—my goodness, I don't know what to
say—except that looks like a moat.

BIRGIT

Ah yes, you have found the Weesageechak Water Slide.
Excellent. The Berlin-based business conglomerate that
we represent is prepared to invest one hundred sixty-four
million dollars towards the creation of this park.

DONALDA

One hundred and sixty-four—what?!

REINHART

I have made this park my life's work. This will be my
legacy.

DONALDA

One hundred and sixty-four … Did I hear you say one
hundred and sixty-four million? Dollars! That's a … that's
a … a lot.

BIRGIT

Possibly one hundred and seventy, depending on the
fluctuation of the Euro and the Canadian dollar, of
course.

DONALDA

Of course. One hundred and seventy million. Dollars.
Why … when … huh?

BIRGIT

Our company has spent the last four years exploring the
possibility and viability of such an endeavour. Otter Lake is
perfect. It has accessibility. It has location. It has a work

force. It has many positive qualities that would make this venture a success. That is why we want to put OjibwayWorld here.

REINHART

Yes, we are very excited about this. I personally have spent the better part of this year designing the park to accentuate and compliment the local terrain. Call it old-fashioned German efficiency but we have left nothing to chance. Look, (*pointing*) I have created a facsimile of the Rocky Mountains.

DONALDA

Right over our garbage dump.

REINHART

And over here, we have arranged for daily caribou migrations.

DONALDA

Right over our other garbage dump. Look, this is all very amazing and overwhelming ... I don't know where to begin ... but first of all, we never had any caribou around here. Or Rocky Mountains. I thought you guys did your research.

BIRGIT

While the theme park itself will be called OjibwayWorld, we will try to incorporate aspects of as many other great and proud First Nations as possible into the design of the project. After all, you are all brothers and sisters, aren't you?

DONALDA

Um, yeah, sure ... I'm sorry if I seem a little unfocussed but this is a lot to just drop on my desk. It's a great idea, amazing in its scope but—oh look, you've put the dog sled rides right next to my house. My cats will love that.

BIRGIT

Obviously, there will be some restructuring involved. We understand the amount of change this will incur. You know what they say, you cannot make a beautiful totem pole without chopping down a tree.

DONALDA
>So ah ... that's what they say, huh? That's ... that's uh ... very clever.

>*BIRGIT pulls a t-shirt out of one of her bags. It has the same totem statement printed on the front.*

BIRGIT
>Yes, we know. It's on our new line of Native themed t-shirts. $19.99 retail.

>*REINHART opens his coat jacket to reveal his t-shirt.*

REINHART
>Mine says *You have a choice. Its either Ojibway ... or the highway.*

DONALDA
>Well, that's also ... very clever.

BIRGIT
>That is what our focus group said. So, what do you think?

DONALDA
>So, what do I think?

BIRGIT
>About our vision. You are the economic development officer here. This proposal could theoretically provide skilled jobs for over three hundred local people. Tens of millions into the local economy for years to come. With the amount of tourism it will generate both nationally and internationally, it is a fabulous opportunity. This park alone could guarantee the financial independence of your community for decades to come.

DONALDA
>It is a fabulous opportunity, isn't it? Yes, it definitely does look that way. What's this section marked Algonquin Park for?

REINHART
>It will be just like Jurassic Park but with ...

DONALDA
>... Native people. You're planning to clone extinct Native people?!

REINHART
No, no. Think animatronic Ojibways.

DONALDA
Wow. A.I. Artificial Indians. Look, this is all amazing. But I need to take this to the Chief and council before I can say any more, 'cause we're going to need some time to figure this all out. It will solve a lot of problems around here, that's for sure. I assume you have all the usual feasibility studies and economic assessments.

BIRGIT takes out several large folders and bound books, dropping them with a thud on DONALDA's desk.

DONALDA
That's a lot.

BIRGIT
I'll get the rest out in the van.

DONALDA
There's more?

BIRGIT
Oh yes. As I said, we've been planning this for some time. We have formulated every possible contingency. Reinhart, I'll need your help with the dolly. Excuse us please.

They exit and DONALDA leafs through all the material, clearly not looking forward to the work ahead of her. She reads one of the marketing files.

DONALDA
OjibwayWorld! It's Ojibway-tastic!

Scene Three

It is morning. TRAILER is sitting in front of his trailer, with a small fire. He is drinking from a cup and looking deep into the fire for answers. It isn't long before a jogging ANGIE stops and joins him, slightly out of breath.

ANGIE

Hey Trailer, how's it going?

TRAILER

Sorry Angie, this is a no running zone. Even fast walking is discouraged around here. It's a safety issue.

ANGIE

Running could save your life someday.

TRAILER

I guess it depends on what's chasing me. I've never understood that, Jogging. Spending all this time and effort to go as fast as you can just to end up back in the same place. It's like dating Pretty Gal. Or the eleventh grade.

ANGIE

It's good for you. Keeps you lean and mean.

TRAILER

So does being broke.

ANGIE

What is it about Native guys and jogging? I've tried to get Andrew into it but he won't even go near a running shoe. I love a good run. Cleans out my system. I've been here for five years now and still can't get enough of this fresh air. I can't believe I spent most of my life in the city.

TRAILER

I lived in a city once.

ANGIE

For how long?

TRAILER

Two years less a day.

ANGIE
You were in jail?

TRAILER
Yeah, but nothing worth bragging about. I prefer to think of it as a career readjustment. Want something to drink?

ANGIE
No, I'm okay. So, what did you do? I mean to end up in jail.

TRAILER
Angie, you're too young to know. Let's just say, love was involved. And that, my dear, is a much longer prison sentence. (*Pause.*) Have you ever wondered about the true nature of love? I mean what it all means? What we're supposed to do? How it makes us act? What's its purpose?

ANGIE
Those are pretty deep questions, Trailer, for a Wednesday morning in Otter Lake. Why so introspective?

TRAILER
Oh, I'm always introspective. Everybody just thinks of me as silly old Trailer. But I'm a pretty introspective guy. I've got introspection coming out of my ears. Like, you know, this one time, I read an article about this guy who said he was part Metis. Isn't that kinda redundant!? How's Andrew? Haven't seen him in a while.

ANGIE
He's good. Didn't you see him yesterday? He said he was going to drop by.

TRAILER
Nah, was out most of the day, trying to take care of some female business.

ANGIE
Donalda?

TRAILER
She'll come around. How come Officer Andrew's not with you? I thought you two were inseparable.

ANGIE

Working. Something big is happening but he won't tell
me what. Something earth-shattering supposedly, but I'll
get it out of him eventually. He's never been very good
with secrets.

TRAILER

How long have you two been going out?

ANGIE

Almost five years now and, you know, that's a long time.
I'm like thinking, wondering, maybe if we're ever going to
get married. A woman thinks about things like that.

TRAILER

Ah Angie, I think you're maybe tapping into one of the
great mysteries of life. In the end, everything comes down
to love. Or the lack of it. Or the search for it. That's why
they invented country music and whiskey.

> TRAILER sighs. ANGIE sighs. Then she reaches over and takes
> a drink from TRAILER's cup. She then makes a face.

ANGIE

What is this?

TRAILER

I don't know. I found it behind the crisper in the fridge.
The label had rotted off. It's okay once you get used to it.

ANGIE

Kinda like love.

TRAILER

Kinda.

> They stare into the fire together. They both sigh.

ANGIE

Okay, now I'm depressed.

TRAILER

Sorry. I have that effect on people occasionally.

ANGIE

I'm gonna walk home now.

> ANGIE shuffles off, downbeat.

TRAILER

Come again.

> *TRAILER sits there, drinking his drink. A few seconds later, OFFICER ANDREW approaches and surveys the rather decrepit location. Then he spots TRAILER.*

ANDREW

Good morning, Trailer. You've been bothering Donalda again, haven't you?

TRAILER

I wasn't bothering Donalda. I was trying to entice her with my charms. The two can sometimes be confused.

ANDREW

Trailer, you've got to stop harassing her at work. At home. At the grocery store. At her gynecologist's?

TRAILER

That one was accidental. I … just ran into her there.

ANDREW

I know you're harmless, Trailer. She knows you're harmless. But really, you're beginning to leave the suburbs of the eccentric for a condo in Creepyville.

TRAILER

Wanna beer?

ANDREW

No, I don't want a beer. Trailer, you've … (*He sniffs.*) What is that smell? Are you cooking?

TRAILER

Oh, that's Kraft Dinner.

ANDREW

Trailer, I've had Kraft Dinner before. That does not smell like Kraft Dinner.

TRAILER

Well, the water pump gave out on me again and I had to improvise.

ANDREW

Improvise?

TRAILER

I'm boiling the noodles in root beer. Hey, it's pretty good. Actually I prefer it in ginger ale but you gotta make do with what you can. Want to try some?

ANDREW

Trailer, that's disgusting. How can you eat that stuff?

TRAILER

What? Now you're Mr. High and Mighty? Just because you've got a gun and—and—socks, you're now too good to eat with the rest of us? I remember the days when you weren't afraid to eat a few wild apples with the rest of us, even though they may have had a few worms in them. That never bothered you then.

ANDREW

Actually, it did.

TRAILER

Come on. Kraft Dinner doesn't get much more exciting than this! Think of it as Indigenous fusion cuisine. People would pay big bucks for it in fancy restaurants.

ANDREW

I did miss breakfast.

TRAILER

Andrew—

ANDREW

I don't believe I'm going to do this—

TRAILER

I can also make you a peanut butter and jelly sandwich, except with just mustard and relish. Hey, Andrew, can you get me a job?

ANDREW

Trailer, you want a job?! Won't that interfere with your *career*?

TRAILER

Oh, I can still play bass in the Road Warriors, but that's only 12 hours a week and I think Pretty Gal wants me to do something else in the remaining 156 hours in the week.

ANDREW
Can't she get you a job?! She is the economic development officer. That's what she gets paid to do.

TRAILER
No, its not right when you have to go to your girlfriend for a job. Not manly.

ANDREW
Donalda's not your girlfriend, Trailer. You really have to remember that. For Christ's sake, she has two kids and was married for eight years.

TRAILER
That's just her way of playing hard to get. She loves me, really she does. I see it in her eyes every time she slams the door. (*An egg timer can be heard going off in the background.*) Oops, le Cuisine de Trailer is just about ready. Come in.

ANDREW
Trailer, were you a cartoon in another life?

They both disappear into the trailer. A few seconds later the TWO GERMANS and DONALDA come wandering by the trailer.

BIRGIT
Yes very good. I like the site. What do you think, Reinhart?

REINHART
Yes, yes, very good. I can see the four-storey teepee video arcade going up here, over there the wigwam cineplex, and that would be the perfect spot for the ILOP, the International Longhouse of Pancakes. It's all coming together. I am quite excited. Aren't you?

BIRGIT
Very. Now what about this structure? It's right in the middle of where the Sweatlodge Spa and Sauna will be.

DONALDA
Yes, the trailer. Well, I'm sure we can get the occupant to move it. Shouldn't be difficult.

BIRGIT

Yes. Good. Do you know the man?

DONALDA

Actually, he's the man who was in my office yesterday.

BIRGIT

Trailer ... right?

DONALDA

Yes, his full name is Fabian Noah.

REINHART

What a unique structure. I'm sorry I don't recognize the architectural style.

DONALDA

It's called rural decay.

REINHART

Is it traditional?

DONALDA

Ever since we signed the treaty. It's been a tradition in Mr. Noah's family for generations.

BIRGIT

Maybe we can chat with the man ...

REINHART

We are right here.

DONALDA

Mr. Noah ... Trailer ... is a rather unusual fellow. I wouldn't advise ...

BIRGIT

Nonsense. As we said last night at the council meeting, we want everybody's support in this venture. Disgruntled members could jeopardize this one hundred seventy million dollar project. Is he an amiable gentleman? Do you have any leverage with the man at all? Any way to possibly influence him?

DONALDA

Oh God ...

> Suddenly TRAILER sticks his head out the door.

29

TRAILER
Pretty Gal. Is that you, Pretty Gal?! You've come back to me!

BIRGIT
Pretty Gal?

DONALDA
That's ... that's ... um.

REINHART
Your traditional Ojibway name?

DONALDA
Yeah, what the hell. Trailer, you remember Birgit Heinze and Reinhart Reinholz.

TRAILER
Hey Beer Gut!

BIRGIT/REINHOLZ
Ahneen, Neechee.

TRAILER
Hey you speak Ojibway?

DONALDA
They're German.

TRAILER
(*knowingly*) Ah.

> *ANDREW steps out of the trailer, still munching on his bowl of noodles.*

ANDREW
Well, I can't say it's the best I've ever had. Can't say it's the worst I've ever had. Can't actually say much.

TRAILER
Like I said. It's better with ginger ale. The taste is much more subtle and the noodles should be more *el dente*. Look, we got guests.

DONALDA
Andrew, what are you doing here?

ANDREW
Your complaint.

BIRGIT

Complaint?

DONALDA

Yes—ah—I was complaining that Trailer here never gets enough visitors. Andrew's just a … a … sweet guy and was here making sure Trailer wasn't lonely.

ANDREW

I was?

TRAILER

You were?

DONALDA

You was and he were.

BIRGIT

Mr. Noah. Have you heard about our project?

TRAILER

No. I have not heard about your project. Evidently nobody visits me, remember? What project would this be?

REINHART

OjibwayWorld!

TRAILER

OjibwayWorld!

REINHART

Doesn't that sound fabulous!?

TRAILER

Well, speaking as somebody who is one hundred percent Ojibway, it sounds like paradise but what does that have to do with me, you and them?

BIRGIT

May we have a moment of your time?

TRAILER

For OjibwayWorld, you may have two. Come. Enter. Sit. Just kick aside whatever isn't moving. Are you hungry? Let me provide you with some rare Ojibway delicacies.

BIRGIT

You are most kind. Thank you.

> *They take turns entering, with DONALDA being last.*

31

TRAILER

I bet you never thought you'd see the inside of my trailer again, did you? 1993 seems almost like yesterday. And you'll be happy to know I've changed the sheets since you were last here. (*to ANDREW*) I told you she was just playing hard to get.

DONALDA

I haven't been to church in twenty years but I have to say it ... Yeah though I walk through the valley of the shadow of death I shall fear no evil ...

She enters, leaving TRAILER and ANDREW.

TRAILER

Do you know what this is about?

ANDREW nods, still eating.

TRAILER

Is there money involved?

Again ANDREW nods. Vigorously.

TRAILER

Enough money that I can get my water pump fixed and boil my Kraft Dinner in water?

Again ANDREW nods.

TRAILER

Well, then, let's see what fortune has brought to my door. Come Andrew, the Creator has seen fit to send two Germans a knockin'. That can only mean good things. I heard an Elder say that once.

They enter the trailer.

Scene Four

Back at ANDREW's office.

ANGIE

They want to call it what?!

ANDREW

OjibwayWorld.

ANGIE

That's ... that's ... obscene!

ANDREW

It's a little eccentric.

ANGIE

It's ... it's ... horrible! That's why you wouldn't tell me,
you bastard. You knew it would upset me ...

ANDREW

—and it is. Now you know why I didn't invite you to the
meeting last night. Anybody, and I'm not mentioning
names, who won't let me watch *Star Trek Voyager* because of
the Native character—

ANGIE

I find him insulting. What's with that silly tattoo? They
never say what nation he's from. If they're gonna use him,
they should explain him and his heritage instead of
making some vague references to his *aboriginality*. I want
to know!

ANDREW

As I was saying. I suspected you wouldn't have the proper
enthusiasm for this idea. You lack vision ... my squeeze-
muffin.

ANGIE

Don't you squeeze-muffin me! I'm the only one with
vision. You approve of this ... this ... travesty?!

ANDREW

It's money. It's jobs. It celebrates our culture, in its own
way. What's not to approve?

ANGIE
It prostitutes our culture. And we're the pimps.

ANDREW
Angie …

ANGIE
And you have the audacity to say you love me.

ANDREW
I'm sorry. I take it back.

ANGIE
And … and … I can't believe the Chief and council approved this.

ANDREW
They've approved it in theory. There's still a lot of paper work and facts and figures to be looked at but essentially, everybody thinks it's a great idea. Except for Trailer, of course. He's a little reluctant. It's that stupid trailer of his. He's a little too protective of it, if you ask me. But Donalda thinks he'll come around.

ANGIE
Trailer's right, and you don't hear people saying that very often.

ANDREW
Look Angie, if the Germans pull this off, this community will be sitting pretty. Germans know what they're doing. They'll have this place running like a … a Volvo.

ANGIE
The Swedes designed the Volvo. You're thinking of a Mercedes-Benz—an expensive and overrated vehicle. Andrew, the Ojibway culture shouldn't be marketed, merchandised, dressed up and auctioned off. Am I the only one who sees this?

ANDREW looks around the room.

ANDREW
Yeah.

ANGIE

Well, I'm not going to let this happen … First pow wows, then casinos, now this … this … horrendously bad idea. There's more to life than money!

ANDREW

Why don't you ask some of the people who don't have any?

At this point, DONALDA enters, carrying some files.

DONALDA

Andrew, could you take a look at …

ANGIE

You! You're the one to blame for all this! You are the one who's responsible for all this insanity …

DONALDA

Me? What did I do? I just came from Burger King.

ANDREW

Angie White, the love of my life, has some issues with OjibwayWorld.

ANGIE

Oh God that's such a stupid name. Donalda, I can't believe you allowed these people into your office.

DONALDA

Actually, you can call me Pretty Gal now.

ANDREW

Pretty Gal? I haven't heard you go by that name in a hell of a long time.

DONALDA

Yeah, I know but the Germans found out I used to be called that and they seem to like it and now that's all they call me.

ANGIE

I've never heard anybody call you Pretty Gal before.

DONALDA

That was ten years and twenty pounds ago. Anyways, like I said, the Germans like it. So, what the hell. There are a lot worse nicknames out there.

ANGIE

So just because the Germans like it, you are just going to roll over and take it?

DONALDA

Since when is being called Pretty Gal rolling over and taking it?

ANGIE

If ... if ... the Germans told you to jump off a bridge, would you?

DONALDA

Well, considering the Germans know practically everything there is to know about Native people, they would more than likely know we never had bridges.

ANDREW

We didn't but I remember reading that the Inca, down in Peru, had a pretty elaborate system of bridges.

DONALDA

And don't forget the Aztecs too.

ANDREW

I'm always forgetting the Aztecs.

ANGIE

Stop it! You're missing my point entirely. These Germans show up on our Reserve, wave a bag of money, and then we all jump through hoops saying how quickly we're prepared to ridicule our heritage.

DONALDA

I don't remember that in the contract. Angie, I know this is all happening so fast. It's amazing. But we have a thirty percent unemployment rate. This time next year, we'll probably be importing people to work. That's a good thing. I know you see this as a form of cultural exploitation, I lost some sleep over it last night too, but the reality is that poverty, substance abuse, and a lack of a focused future can be far more damaging. In the end, I think this is a good thing.

ANDREW

So do I. Practically everybody wants it. Except you.

ANGIE

And Trailer. There's got to be others here that feel the same way we do.

DONALDA

Maybe, but its still going to get done. OjibwayWorld will be born. It's official.

ANGIE

No. Nelson Mandela said no. Rosa Parks said no. Martin Luther King said no. They stood alone. They knew better. I will be heard. Now excuse me, I have toy canoes to unpack.

ANGIE storms out.

DONALDA

Does she know all the people she mentioned are black? And she isn't.

ANDREW

I'll break it to her later. So, Pretty Gal, what can I do for you?

DONALDA

These are the proposed security requirements the Germans have anticipated. Are you going to take the job?

ANDREW

Probably.

DONALDA

Security Chief of OjibwayWorld.

ANDREW

I do love that word, Chief.

DONALDA

Double the responsibility.

ANDREW

Double the pay.

DONALDA

Double the stress.

ANDREW
> Double the vacation time. And what about you?

DONALDA
> I don't know. On-Site Liaison and Chief Cultural Advisor.
> Awfully big titles.

ANDREW
> Between my new title and yours, those Germans sure like
> to use the word Chief a lot, don't they?

DONALDA
> This is gonna change Otter Lake forever, Andrew.
> Nothing's ever going to be the same.

ANDREW
> You said that the first time you dyed your hair. Well,
> change is good. Isn't it?

DONALDA
> That's what the Theory of Evolution tells us. Anything
> stagnant dies.

ANDREW
> So you're saying it's either OjibwayWorld or death? That's
> awfully limited.

DONALDA
> Don't listen to me. My point of view might be a little
> slanted. I just got my credit card statement. Now that's
> bleak.

Scene Five

Outside TRAILER's trailer. Once more TRAILER is staring into the fire on the dark night. Occasionally he sips from a cup.

TRAILER
What to do? What to do?

And for no reason, he lets out a loud, long, mournful coyote/wolf howl.

TRAILER
Nope. Didn't help.

BIRGIT wanders by, making notes on her clipboard. She spots TRAILER and approaches.

BIRGIT
Ah, Mr. Trailer. Good evening. Enjoying the night air I see.

TRAILER
Yep.

BIRGIT
It is truly beautiful country around here. You are lucky to live here.

TRAILER.
Yep.

BIRGIT
I have a small two-bedroom apartment in Berlin. Overlooking the train station.

TRAILER doesn't say anything.

BIRGIT
Still thinking about our offer?

TRAILER
Yep.

BIRGIT
Have you changed your mind?

TRAILER
Nope.

BIRGIT

I see. Your fire looks lovely. Mind if I join you?

TRAILER

Nope.

BIRGIT

What kind of wood are you burning?

TRAILER

Thirteen-year-old picnic table. If you prefer, Miss Beer Gut, I have some old porch wood. The paint makes the smoke smell sweeter.

BIRGIT

No, this is quite lovely. And just Birgit is fine.

TRAILER

Just Trailer then.

BIRGIT

I understand your Christian name is Fabian. That's a lovely name.

TRAILER

Thanks. My mother and father met playing in a rock band. Named all their kids after their favourite singer or group.

BIRGIT

Really?!

TRAILER

Yep. There's about ten of us, from my youngest brother, Prince, to my oldest sister, Cher.

BIRGIT

NO traditional Indian names?

TRAILER

Got a cousin named Kahliga.

BIRGIT

Interesting. Have you lived here all your life, Trailer?

TRAILER

That's what they tell me, though I cannot personally vouch for my first couple of years. And you are from Berlin, over there in Germany ...

BIRGIT

Actually I was born in Marburg. It's a lovely town. They
named a strain of the Ebola virus after it, after it was
identified in a lab there.

TRAILER

And now you're sitting halfway across the world, on a
Canadian Reserve, sitting around a campfire, talking to
Trailer. Is this a good thing or a bad thing?

BIRGIT

Oh, very good. You must understand, Trailer. This theme
park has been a life long dream for me. Ever since I was a
young girl I have loved Native people. I read all the old
Winnitou and Shatterhand stories. I even joined one of
the clubs where we dressed up like Indians and held our
own pow wows. I made my own buckskin dress, if you can
believe it.

TRAILER

German Indians and pow wows? I guess that's what they
call globalization. But why us? Why the Ojibway? I mean,
let's face it, the Apache, Cherokees, the Lakota, the
Mohawks ... they're all better known than us Ojibway. I
see LakotaLand or MohawkMall before I see
OjibwayWorld. I'm surprised you guys have even heard
of us.

BIRGIT

That's because I personally am responsible for focussing
on the Ojibway. Yes, my corporation was more interested
in Lakota Land, I will admit it. But the Ojibway, there is
just something so special about your people. Something
that reached out and grabbed me and wouldn't let go.

TRAILER

Heard the same thing said about my cooking. Or maybe it
was our beadwork. Nobody does beadwork like us. I don't
like to brag but ...

BIRGIT

I know, I know. I have three beaded vests, one jacket,
sixteen porcupine quill boxes, some moose tuft paintings

41

and my pride and joy is the birchbark bitten wall hanging. What can I say, you people really know how to bite trees.

TRAILER

Yeah, it's an Ojibway thing. And people are going to come to this—OjibwayWorld?

BIRGIT

Thousands. Tens of thousands. Maybe hundreds of thousands. We have anticipated a world wide marketing plan for those in Germany and other parts of the world intrigued by visions of Native people. You underestimate the appeal of your heritage, my good friend. Trust me, once we have built it, they will come.

TRAILER

You know, this trailer is very old. This new vision of yours wants to wipe it out of existence. Does that make good business sense?

BIRGIT

We will give you fair compensation.

TRAILER

Money. I could use the money I suppose. I could get a new water pump and stop brushing my teeth in pickle brine. But you know, the more money you have, the more you spend, and the more you need to make. It's a vicious circle, that, unfortunately, might end up with me getting a job. And according to recent developments, evidently I need to get one.

BIRGIT

A job? You are looking for a job you say? What exactly do you do, my friend?

TRAILER

I—guess you could say I'm in the entertainment business. I like putting on a good show. The stage is my life.

BIRGIT

Well, how fortunate, for both of us. Maybe I can sweeten the pot, my good friend Trailer.

TRAILER

(*nervous*) You can see my pot from here?

BIRGIT

Let me throw a position title at you. A title and the job: OjibwayWorld's Chief Entertainment Development Coordinator and Artistic Producer.

TRAILER

What do all those fancy words mean, exactly?

BIRGIT

It means you, Trailer Noah, would be responsible for all entertainment and productions. You would produce them, write them, direct them, or hire other people if you wanted, whatever you consider would best showcase the Aboriginal spirit of your people.

TRAILER

But I'm just a bass player. Call it a hunch but this may be a little over my head.

BIRGIT

Nonsense. I started out bringing coffee. You, Trailer Fabian Noah, are only limited by your imagination and ability.

TRAILER

… limited only by my imagination and ability you say. Pretty Gal had a much longer list. Well, I don't know … this is a huge, life-altering decision. I should talk it over with my family and—and I sure wish Elvis was around.

BIRGIT

Elvis, the King of Rock 'n' Roll?

TRAILER

No, Elvis the Chief of Otter Lake. He's my brother. He left today for a conference.

> *TRAILER takes a sip from his cup.*

BIRGIT

May I?

TRAILER

Yeah, if you want. It's just rye with some coke I had left over from my cereal.

BIRGIT

And what's that floating in it?

TRAILER

Oh that, well I had no ice cubes, water problems, so I threw in some frozen peas and corn. Does the job if you don't mind a lumpy texture in your drink.

BIRGIT

How unusual.

TRAILER

But nutritious.

BIRGIT

Is this a common Otter Lake practice?

TRAILER

Oh sure. I saw it bitten on a piece of birchbark once.

She samples some of it. Her face gives her reaction.

TRAILER

Well, you know, there is something I've always wanted to do, show business wise, but never had the guts to even seriously think about. It would be big. Amazing. Never seen before

BIRGIT

OjibwayWorld demands something big, amazing and never seen before. It sounds perfect already. What is it?

TRAILER

Five words. *Dances With Wolves—The Musical!*

Scene Six

ANGIE is going through some files on ANDREW's desk. She is not happy.

ANGIE

Ride the Okanagan Toboggan. The Malicite Drink 'n' Eat. The Shuswap Drop and Shop? I think I'm gonna be sick.

She shuffles through some more papers.

Plans for a music festival called *Lakota-palooza.* I am gonna be sick.

ANDREW is standing in the doorway.

ANDREW

I think those are private.

ANGIE

What are these doing on your desk?

ANDREW

That's a long story. Why are you so interested in them?

ANGIE

I have a meeting tomorrow with Trailer's brother, the lawyer.

ANDREW

Simon?

ANGIE

No, Garfunkel. The other lawyer. I am going to be the conscience of this community if it kills me. Andrew, why do you have all these documents?!

ANDREW

And thus Andrew spoke his dying words. The Germans have offered me a job.

ANGIE

A job!? What kind of job?

ANDREW

With OjibwayWorld. As head of security.

ANGIE

But you're a police officer. You have a job.

45

ANDREW

Well yes but, I could use the extra money. The Caribbean is calling, remember?

ANGIE

You already make good money. Why do you need extra money?

ANDREW

Well, I am broke.

ANGIE

You are not broke. I know exactly how much money you make and have. You're just making excuses.

ANDREW

No. I really am broke.

ANGIE

You can't be ... Andrew, what's going on here? Is there something about you I should know? Something I've managed to overlook for the past five years? Something expensive—and icky?

ANDREW

Angie, the reason I'm broke is I spent all my money to buy this.

He holds out a small black box, ring size. Then he opens it.

ANGIE

It's a ... it's a ...

ANDREW

Come on. You can say it.

ANGIE

A ring. You got me a ring. That's why you're broke. (*Pause.*) Why did you get me a ring?

ANDREW

It's called a proposal.

ANGIE

Well, I haven't heard any proposal. I see a ring but I believe there is usually a verbal question that accompanies these things.

ANDREW

Right. Okay, Angie White, will you marry me?

ANGIE

How many carats?

ANDREW

More than enough to make a little Indian girl happy.
(*Pause.*) Uh, in my experience, there's usually some form
of affirmative response returned.

ANGIE

Your experience?! You've proposed to someone before?

ANDREW

Can I have the ring back please?

ANGIE

Man, I'm gonna have to make you a lot tougher. Nope I'm
gonna keep it cause I'm gonna marry you. Happy?

ANDREW

I don't know anymore.

    ANGIE hugs and kisses ANDREW, then realizes something.

ANGIE

Hey, wait a minute. Did you just tell me you were offered a
job at OjibwayWorld? You turned it down, right?

ANDREW

If I turn it down, I'll have to give back the ring.

ANGIE

Give the ... But ... its so pretty. Look at it sparkle.

ANDREW

That sparkle is more than a humble Rez cop can afford.

ANGIE

You can always sell your car ...

ANDREW

It's the police car, Angie. I sell it, I go to jail.

ANGIE

But Andrew, OjibwayWorld ...? You'll be working for the
Aboriginal Wal-Mart. It's evil. It will be like parking cars
for the Anti-Christ.

ANDREW
Okay, give me the ring back.

ANGIE
I guess evil is a subjective term. If you can sleep nights, knowing you work for them ...

ANDREW
Oh I and we will sleep very well. The new house I'm planning to build will have air conditioning. Heated tile floors. Hot tub. And, hold on to your panties my love, a personal gym. You can pump iron, Stairmaster, sweat and grunt your way to happiness. You'll be able to run as long as you want without leaving the comfort of your own home.

ANGIE
I would have my own gym? Really? Oh Andrew, I really love you now. But what about my ideals? My convictions? My beliefs? I shouldn't let this ring buy me off, should I? I mean, I am a woman of the new millennium. Things like this are so cliché, silly, passé ... right? Andrew, I'm confused.

ANDREW
Angel muffin, you are putting far too much thought into a question that normally has a one word answer. Let me up the ante. I took the job on one condition. You are always going on about diabetes being rampant in the Native community. The level of obesity. The lack of decent health programs. The Germans are willing to build a wellness centre. Here in the village. Right beside Todd's Lard and Spam Barn. Let's see you argue with that.

ANGIE
A wellness centre, here. IN the village? That's playing dirty.

ANDREW
They're not all bad. Does that take the edge off the Germans and OjibwayWorld? Should I be looking for a tux?

ANGIE

What the hell! A wellness centre is a wellness centre. I will
take it as a good omen. And can you get them to use
Anishnaabe instead of Ojibway? That is the more correct
term these days.

ANDREW

I'll see what I can do.

ANGIE

Hmmm, Angie Kakina. How does that sound?

ANDREW

Beats Angie White.

ANGIE

When do you start your new job?

ANDREW

In three months.

ANGIE

Talk about sleeping with the enemy.

ANDREW

Who says I'm gonna let you sleep? You know, maybe we
can get married at the Chippewa Chapel. I can get us a
discount.

Scene Seven

*TRAILER sitting by his campfire, with a guitar or bass. He is
in the process of writing a song.*

TRAILER

It all began when I rode my horse across the civil war.
Back then I was known as a lieutenant John Dunbar.
Since then I have stood naked on the plains and won
my fame,
I am a white man no longer. Dances With Wolves is
my Name.

Wind in his Hair is my friend, and Stands with a Fist
my wife.
I have hunted Tatonka and found the meaning of life.
Memories of my former life now leave me filled with
shame.
I am a white man no longer. Dances with Wolves is
my name.

I am a white man no longer. Dances with Wolves is
my name.

Lights go down.
End of Act One.

ACT TWO

Scene One

It is one year later. It is a week before the opening of OjibwayWorld and the tempo of the community has been sped up several notches. A production number of Dances With Wolves—The Musical. One or two performers in Vegas-influenced Lakota make-up and clothing.

PERFORMERS

They came from the East, looking for something.
Even they did know not what
Strangers from afar with even stranger ways.
They soon changed things a lot.

Now they're here to stay, forever it seems
Getting under our feet.
It seems times have changed, for all of us
To them we're nothing but meat.

Strangers became friends until the very end.
Though they couldn't tell it was the gates of Hell.

Chorus (repeat twice.)
Lakota, Lakota, they shoulda been, coulda woulda shoulda
But they're not.
Dark as the Earth, proud as the skies,
Noble like the wolf, as the eagle flies.
Lakota, Lakota, they shoulda been, coulda woulda shoulda
But they're not.

Scene Two

Characters now dress in reverse. TRAILER, DONALDA and ANDREW are now better-dressed, while REINHART dresses more casually with the odd bit of Otter Lake/Native apparel. Stress is in the air. REINHART and DONALDA enter her office.

DONALDA

I can't believe it's almost done. So much in so little time. You guys are amazing.

REINHART

Yes we are. But it could not have been done without your help.

Pretty Gal, my time here, working on this project, with you—and the rest of the community has meant so much to me. I feel reborn.

DONALDA

That's good. Reborn is good.

REINHART

I hope you have enjoyed our time together just as much.

DONALDA

Yeah, it's been quite the ride. What will you do once it's open? I mean as architect, your job will be finished once OjibwayWorld is open.

REINHART

I do not know. I am weighing my options. There is not much for me back in Germany. I am looking for possibilities. Pretty Gal, I must ask you something.

DONALDA

Oh please don't.

REINHART

I must know—

DONALDA

Where's Birgit? I really would like to know where she is.

REINHART

Birgit? She is off making sure the pemmican is being
made properly. Evidently the berry/buffalo mixture was
inaccurate.

DONALDA

That sounds like Birgit. You two sure are different. How
did you meet?

REINHART

We met at a Free Leonard Peltier concert in Kiel and then
again at a Native film festival in Stuttgart. Birgit and I
share the same dream but it came to us separately. She
found the Native experience in Germany. I, on the other
hand, went to the root source. I have spent much of the
last decade travelling to Native communities, learning,
absorbing, sweating. Some of the best memories I have are
of playing bingo, filing land claims, gutting caribou.
Simple everyday things like that.

DONALDA

Have you two ever, like, fooled around?

REINHART

No. Birgit's tastes for the exotic sickens me. My tastes are
much more simple. Come, I want to show you something.
We put it up this weekend.

*REINHART moves her to the window and points to something
off in the distance.*

REINHART

Is it not impressive?

DONALDA

Holy—That is huge! That thing must be easily, thirty or
forty metres across.

REINHART

Actually, it is forty-four metres, forty-four centimetres in
diameter.

DONALDA

That has got to be the biggest damn dreamcatcher I have
ever seen!

REINHART

The webbing will be made with interconnecting laser beams!

DONALDA

Why forty-four metres, forty-four centimetres exactly? Some sort of architectural, drafting, blue-printy type thing?

REINHART

No. It is to honour the number four that your people hold in such high esteem. The four directions. The four seasons. The four parts of the plant. The four races of man. I thought you would have gotten the symbolism of it immediately.

DONALDA

Oh yeah. Of course. The number four. Tell me again, what are you going to do with such a huge dreamcatcher?

REINHART.

Silly girl, you know the relevance and purpose of the dreamcatcher, I don't have to tell you something you and your people have shared spiritually for thousands of years.

DONALDA

I'm one-eighth Irish. You can tell that part.

REINHART

Very well. The legend of the dreamcatcher states that it is to be given to the mother of a newborn baby or a newly married couple, to hang in the window so all the bad dreams will stick to the webbing and be burnt away by the morning sun. The good dreams pass through. Well, OjibwayWorld is our baby, our collective child. Not only will it be good for the park, but it also pays homage to your people and their beliefs. That is why it is positioned over the eastern entrance.

DONALDA

… the eastern entrance …?

REINHART

Again you tease me, Pretty Gal. The morning sun! It has to be in the window facing the dawn. The east. You are just doing this to test me, are you not?

DONALDA

You caught me. Other than the giant laser beam dream-catcher sticking out of the forest, how is the rest of the opening looking?!

REINHART

Oh, very well. The Premier, the Prime Minister, several local dignitaries, all the tribal elders have been invited to next week's opening. All is good in the world.

DONALDA

When's the last time you slept?!

REINHART

Who can sleep?! This is exciting! This is history! We have actually managed to pull this off in only twelve months. Do you realize what an accomplishment that is?

DONALDA

Yes, in more ways than one. German time meeting Indian time. I'm surprised there wasn't a rupture in the space-time continuum. You should get some sleep. Who's ever heard of a frazzled German?

REINHART

Yes, I suppose you are right. But one thing first, Pretty Gal. Not everybody has been as wonderful as you. There have been mutterings of discontent in the community. Some of your apples refuse to fall from the tree and ripen.

DONALDA

Angie means well. Her heart's in the right place but she can get a little over excited.

REINHART

Calling Immigration to deport us might not be viewed by some as being *a little over-excited.*

DONALDA

Andrew talked to her about that. Really, he did!

55

REINHART
> And our parent company does not dump nuclear waste in
> kindergarten sand boxes.

DONALDA
> She can be quite creative, can't she?

REINHART
> And schnitzel is not made from kittens.
>
> *Suddenly a very changed TRAILER bursts into the room,*
> *talking on a cell phone. He is less a downtrodden bassist,*
> *and more a frustrated, on-the-edge theatrical producer. His*
> *energy level has tripled.*

TRAILER
> Jesus H!!! I can't believe you're doing this to me. This
> can't be happening! You're ruining me, dude! Killing me.
> I will have your job for this, you idiot. I really need this
> done and I won't let you screw this up. It's too important.
> So listen to me good, are you listening? For the last time,
> no friggin' mushrooms. If that pizza has one, solitary,
> piece of fungus sitting there surrounded by cheese,
> pepperoni and bacon, there will be lawsuits involved. I
> swear this by every god that is worshipped. Do I make
> myself clear! Good. Thank you. Oh, and don't forget the
> garlic bread.
>
> *He hangs up.*

TRAILER
> (*to DONALDA*) My brother says hello.

DONALDA
> How is Bono?

TRAILER
> I didn't ask. Look, where are we with the amphitheatre?

REINHART
> It will be finished in two days.

TRAILER
> Good. I need it for the dress rehearsals. Goddamn actors
> can't do anything right.

DONALDA
Ah yes. *Dances with Wolves—The Musical.*

TRAILER
Did you know actors have unions!? Directors, stage
managers too! Even musicians!? Unions?! I hate unions!?
They don't trust me?! I'm Ojibway. I'm very trustworthy.
Ask anybody. We're more trustworthy than the Amish!

DONALDA
Union problems?

TRAILER
No kidding. They want me to up the salaries because of
something called a special risk clause.

DONALDA
What is that?

TRAILER
Ah, the scared little actors are afraid of the buffalo.

DONALDA
What buffalo?

TRAILER
For the buffalo stampede. It'll be great. I've got practically
every working unionized buffalo signed up for the
production. Which reminds me ... excuse me.

*TRAILER takes out his cell phone again and makes a quick
call. He moves off to the side.*

DONALDA
He seems a little stressed.

REINHART
We are all a little stressed. I have seen some of the
rehearsals. He is doing a fine job.

DONALDA
He actually got real buffalo?! Those things are huge.

REINHART
He seems to know what he's doing. At one point he
seriously considered flying in some actual Pawnee from
the U.S. for the internecine warfare sequence. He was
striving for authenticity. Unfortunately, he couldn't find

any that could ride a horse, shoot a bow and arrow and sing a tender love ballad, all at the same time. We were all disappointed.

TRAILER

(*speaking loudly*) That's all the buffalo you could find?! Thirteen! That's it! Geez, my heart. My heart—Listen, beaver nuts, that's not nearly enough. Thirteen buffalo is not a stampede. That's not majestic, its anaemic. That won't even raise a decent cloud of dust. I've got to have better than that. I need more buffalo. I've gotta have more buffalo. A lot more. And ones that can run. Gallop. The ones we got in two days ago … I'm not sure they can run. They just stand there. Looking at me. (*Pause.*) I'm serious. They all got this *you killed off my ancestors and you expect me to run for you?* look in their eyes. It's unnerving. (*Pause.*) Just get me as many fast running buffalo as you can. Go outside the regular buffalo unions if you have to. See if there are any scab buffalos or black market ones.

DONALDA

Having buffalo problems, Trailer?

TRAILER

Who doesn't? Hey, has anybody seen that giant spiderweb thing out back?

DONALDA

It's a dreamcatcher

> *While still on the phone, he takes a quick peak out the window.*

TRAILER

Yeah, I guess so.

DONALDA

It's made of laser beams.

TRAILER

That so? Hmm, that explains all the dead, scorched seagulls. Ah, they're not answering. I gotta take care of this. See you later. I'm outta here.

> *TRAILER exits.*

DONALDA

There's something different about him.

REINHART

Come. There is something else I must show you—

DONALDA

Oh what is it now? Another exhibit? Another ride? More pseudo-Indigenous games and theme ... things?!

REINHART

No. That. I saw it there this morning when I went out to greet the morning sun, as is the custom of your people. You must join me some morning. But first, please tell me if that is what I think it is?

He points out the window and DONALDA takes a look.

DONALDA

That looks like a blockade.

REINHART

A one woman blockade.

DONALDA

Well, we Native women have always believed size doesn't really matter. Angie?

REINHART

I believe so. Have you managed to maintain your friendship with her?

DONALDA

For the most part. She owes me seventy-five bucks.

REINHART

Perhaps you could have a word with her. It is not exactly good business to have a protester picketing the front gates of a theme park a week before opening. I'm an architect, not a publicist, but something tells me it's not necessarily a good thing. Bad karma.

DONALDA

I'll have a word with her.

REINHART

Maybe several. We do not want any incidents.

DONALDA

What do you define as an incident?

REINHART

Anything that Birgit could fire people over.

DONALDA

You are aware that a lot of us are kind of overwhelmed by all this. A year ago we were just a small sleepy little Reserve stuck out in the middle of nowhere. Now we're about to become a major, international tourist attraction. We've had CBC, CNN, ABC, CBS, APTN, CTV, MSNBC, M.O.U.S.E. That's a lot to adjust to in just twelve months.

REINHART

Success can be a harsh mistress. Have you lost your enthusiasm?

DONALDA

No. Just the peace and quiet.

REINHART

Would you like me to come with you?

DONALDA

No, that would be like taking a cat into a kennel. Let me talk to her.

REINHART

I have the utmost confidence in you.

DONALDA leaves the office.

Scene Three

Just outside ObjibwayWorld, a little mini-blockade,
population one: ANGIE. DONALDA approaches.

DONALDA

Hey Angie.

ANGIE

Hey Pretty Gal. (*Pause.*) Did the Germans send you? Am I
Poland?

There is an awkward silence.

DONALDA

This isn't going to accomplish anything, you know. You
are one small woman against a huge corporation. I heard
about the petition you were taking around.

ANGIE

You can change the world with only fourteen signatures.

DONALDA

It and you are too little, too late. Knock, knock, reality
would like to have a word with you.

ANGIE

Pretty Gal, remember a few years back when you and me
went to that hockey tournament and got in a fight with
those women from Dead Rat River?

DONALDA

Unfortunately yes. I can still dislocate my finger at will. I
still maintain that woman didn't say *Andrew was hot.* She
said *Andrew was a cop.*

ANGIE

It doesn't matter. You were there when I needed you. I
need you now. Hey Pretty Gal, why don't you join me?
OjibwayWorld is not the world of the Ojibways. It's some
genetically modified, bastardized, hybrid, freak show. As
Native women, it's our obligation, our right, to protect
and preserve the culture. Why am I the only one who
knows that?! This should be your fight! I've only been
here five years, you've been here all your life.

DONALDA is quiet for a moment.

DONALDA

Have you seen the forty-four metre, forty-four centimetre laser dreamcatcher? Its ... big. It's hideous. It's sooo not Otter Lake. Not the one I know.

ANGIE

That's what I've been talking about!!!

DONALDA

You know, things have been getting a little out of hand. In the beginning, I thought it was a great idea. Work. Improved self image. International connections. But people have changed, Angie. Take Trailer, he barely talks to me anymore. When he does, it's to bitch, complain, ask for an increase in his production budget, or to fire somebody.

ANGIE

Come on, Pretty Gal, just a little bit further.

DONALDA

Great philosophers have said that either you're part of the problem, or part of the solution. I've sold my soul and I want to buy it back. I have a Lexus. I have a pool. I have a nineteenth-century squash blossom turquoise necklace from the Taos Pueblo in New Mexico. Where the hell am I going to wear a seven-pound squash blossom necklace? Somewhere along the way, we strayed off the path. I have all these ... these ... things but spiritually, I'm empty. Do you know what I'm saying, Angie?

ANGIE

Oh Pretty Gal, you're making me hot.

DONALDA

Angie, I renounce OjibwayWorld!

ANGIE

That's fabulous, Pretty Gal!

DONALDA

No. My name is Donalda.

ANGIE
Actually, I like Pretty Gal better.

DONALDA
Really?!

ANGIE
Yeah. Less masculine. And really, you need all the help
you can get.

DONALDA
But I've always thought ... what?

ANGIE
So, what do we do now? In our battle against the mega-
corporation known as OjibwayWorld?

DONALDA
There's only so much we can do. It opens next week.
Everything is built. It's all set and ready to go. There's one
hundred and seventy million dollars on the other side of
that fence. What have we got?

ANGIE
Determination? Spiritual righteousness? Moral
superiority?

DONALDA
Against one hundred and seventy million dollars?! We're a
little out-manned. Or out-womaned as the case might be.
There's a lot of money riding on this theme park, Angie.
And money has a tendency to make people a little near-
sighted and a lot insane.

ANGIE
So what?

DONALDA
Angie, you should see all the money they plan to make
just from the stuffed mascot dolls. This corporation
expects to pull in about nine million a year within five
years of start up.

ANGIE

That is a lot of toy canoes—Oh come on, Pretty Gal, screw them and their money. You know one Ojibway woman is worth a dozen men, Native or non-Native.

DONALDA

Wonderful. For this corporation, that narrows it down to about three thousand on payroll. Half of them lawyers.

ANGIE

I see your point. We need to recruit. Become a movement. Go on a long march or find a bay full of pigs or something. Hey, why don't you see if you can pull Trailer over to our side again? He is kinda sweet on you.

DONALDA

Unless I suddenly gained twenty-five hundred pounds and develop some short horns, he wouldn't notice me.

ANGIE

If you can't bowl him over with logic, use some of those feminine wiles of yours.

DONALDA

Angie, my feminine wiles are buried somewhere deep in my closet with my Wham records and leg warmers. They are out of date and very dusty.

ANGIE

Come on, Pretty Gal, it's our last resort. Fight evil with evil. Just bat your eyes or show some cleavage. You must be able to do something. Somehow you did manage to have two kids.

DONALDA

What happened to all your feminist rhetoric?

ANGIE

In the struggle against superior numbers, one has to embrace all potential weaponry to achieve one's just cause. Sad but true. Besides, with Indian men, contemporary feminist theory is a pamphlet. Cleavage is the *Encyclopaedia Britannica*. Now what about Trailer?

DONALDA
    What about Andrew?
ANGIE
    He's pretty far over.
DONALDA
    I thought you said he listens to you.
ANGIE
    That was before I promised to behave when they put up
    the wellness centre.
DONALDA
    What are you doing here then?
ANGIE
    I just found out that old saying is true, be careful what you
    ask for, you might get it. The wellness centre is planning
    classes in Anishnaabe aerobics, called Anishnaabics.
    Instead of pilates, its now Anishnaates. They don't give up.
    Look at the logo of the centre, it's an eagle eating a
    bratwurst. I don't care what I promised Andrew. I had to
    do something. I just hope he'll listen to me.
DONALDA
    Gonna bring out the pamphlet or the encyclopaedia?
ANGIE
    I don't know yet. Depends if he's in a reading mood or
    not.

Scene Four

An unhappy TRAILER is in his office, talking with BIRGIT.

BIRGIT

We cannot have any delays. Everything is set to go. You must deal with it.

TRAILER

But the buffalo …

BIRGIT

I do not care about the buffalo.

TRAILER

I care about the buffalo. We managed to get another twenty-five in, for the big stampede scene.

BIRGIT

Well then, what's the problem?

TRAILER

I don't think they like me. They're looking at me funny. All of them. Staring with those beady little eyes. Makes me nervous.

BIRGIT

They are noble but dumb animals. Don't take it personally.

TRAILER

Seriously. The buffalo don't like me. And as an Aboriginal person, that can't be a good sign. I don't mind being ignored by moose, or snubbed by deer. But buffalo …?

BIRGIT

Didn't they come from a farm owned by a White person? Maybe you are just the first Aboriginal person they have ever met. Maybe they are waiting for you to put some tobacco down to honour their spirit.

TRAILER

You guys really do your research, don't you?

BIRGIT

Of course. Now, I have heard continuing rumours about some discontent within the community.

TRAILER

What do you want me to do about it? I've got my hands full dealing with the buffalo, actors, musicians and one cranky props person. Not only that, next week we're starting the workshop on the Cirque du Billy Jack. I'm sleeping four hours a night as it is!

BIRGIT

We're all getting less sleep. But once things open and quiet down, it will get back to normal. In the meantime, continue doing the excellent job you are doing. Before I forget, I am having a celebratory dinner tonight in advance of the opening. I will be expecting you.

TRAILER

Me? Should I bring anything.

BIRGIT

Just a taste for the exotic.

DONALDA knocks at the door and enters.

DONALDA

Everybody working hard, I see.

BIRGIT

Yes.

TRAILER

Pretty Gal, do you know anything about buffalo?

DONALDA

They have great wings.

BIRGIT

Ah, aboriginal humour. Earthy, pun-oriented, often scatological in nature. Excellent. You may continue. I must go. Seven o'clock tonight. Do not be late, Trailer. I would not be happy.

BIRGIT exits. DONALDA undoes her top button while TRAILER isn't looking.

DONALDA
What did she want?

TRAILER
Evidently I'm invited to dinner. Some exotic German dish I think. Maybe she's homesick for some sausage or something.

DONALDA
Are you going?

TRAILER
She's the boss. Gotta keep her happy, especially since there are rumours of discontent.

DONALDA
What did you tell her?

TRAILER
Nothing. I don't know anything. Hey, we're casting for the new Billy Jack workshop. Can you do a crescent kick?

DONALDA
Not after two children and three decades of bannock. Look Trailer, I need to talk to you about something. This discontent thing … there's some logic to it.

TRAILER
I don't care. Do you know how much money I've made so far? Once we moved the trailer, I dug up under it, put in a basement. Took out those old plywood walls and siding and put in brick. Brand new floors and roofing. Added two additional rooms and a whole bunch of other extras. I now have four different types of water coming out of my kitchen taps—soda water, mineral water, filtered water and distilled water. That's what OjibwayWorld has done for me.

DONALDA
Sounds like it's not your trailer anymore. You've renovated it so much, there's nothing left there of what used to be.

TRAILER
Yes there is. Me. By the way, the top button of your blouse is undone.

DONALDA

Oh, thanks. You're not the same either, Trailer.

TRAILER

You want to know what else is true?! Everything you used to say about me ... you were right. Now look at me. I have something to do. I have a future. I'm wrestling life to the floor and ...

DONALDA

... and choking the very life out of it. When's the last time you played your bass or played with the Road Warriors?

TRAILER

We all gotta grow up sometime. Now if you'll excuse me, I have some buffalo issues to deal with.

DONALDA

Trailer?

TRAILER

What?

DONALDA pauses for a moment.

DONALDA

For a second, I thought there was something I wanted to ask you, but I guess not. Good luck with your show. I'm sure it will be fabulous.

TRAILER

I'll make sure you get front row seats. And don't worry, Donalda, everything will be fine.

DONALDA

You called me Donalda.

TRAILER

That is your name, isn't it?

DONALDA

Hey Trailer, wanna go for a beer some time?

TRAILER

Who has time?

TRAILER exits. DONALDA goes to the window and watches him walk away.

DONALDA

Bye … Fabian. Wow. That's a whole lot of buffalo. I hope Angie is doing better.

Scene Five

ANGIE is still at the blockade, writing in large letters on a sign. It says Welcome to OjibwayWorld: Stop exploiting the Third World. *Content, she sticks it into the ground with great satisfaction. ANDREW saunters in.*

ANDREW

You know, technically, that's incorrect. If you want to be precise, we're the fourth world—an oppressed nation within a nation.

ANGIE

How do you know that?

ANDREW

The Germans told me. Nice place for a blockade. No ditches, burnt out school busses or Molotov cocktails though.

ANGIE

They're hard to make with beer.

ANDREW

You know we are getting married next month? Call me an old-fashioned romantic but it would be kinda nice to see some love and warmth in those eyes. Any chance?

ANGIE

There's always a chance, Andrew. The universe is made up of chances. So a positive answer to your question is in direct proportion to the possibility of you seeing the light, coming to your senses, renouncing evil and joining our righteous cause. What are those chances?

ANDREW

As usual, I'm stuck between a rock and an Ojibway woman. Angie, my love, I hate to tell you this but you have to remove this blockade or whatever you want to call it, and promise me that you will not harass the employees, employers, and any of the tourists that will soon start pouring in here.

ANGIE

The Germans sent you, huh? What happened to this self-government argument that's been raging for twenty years? We've left the Canadian government for the Germans? Andrew, do you love me?

ANDREW

Very much.

ANGIE

And here we stand, on different sides of the argument. If worst came to worse, would you take me into custody?

ANDREW

Angie, don't ask me that.

ANGIE

I am asking you that.

BIRGIT and REINHART enter the area.

BIRGIT

Ah, Ms White. Exercising your solitary viewpoint, I see. Mr. Kakina, I assume you've informed her of the situation.

REINHART

Please, Ms White, won't you reconsider? We Germans are very good at negotiating.

He offers her a chocolate bar.

REINHART

Some Swiss chocolate perhaps?

BIRGIT

Nonsense. We've tried. Ms. White, I have here a written resolution from the Chief and Council demanding you vacate the premises.

ANGIE

No.

BIRGIT

Very well. Mr. Kakina, if you please …

ANGIE

If you please what? Andrew, what's going on?

ANDREW

Angie, I love you. Just remember that. Please.

BIRGIT
Mr. Kakina!

ANDREW
This is my fiancé, Ms Heinze. There must be some other
way.

BIRGIT
Yes, there is. Total capitulation. Ms White?

ANGIE
Andrew?

ANDREW
Reinhart?

REINHART
Birgit …

BIRGIT
Now that roll call has been taken, if you please.

*Indecisive and miserable, ANDREW wrestles with what he
must do.*

ANDREW
Angie, they want me to take you into custody for
trespassing and creating a public disturbance.

BIRGIT
Exactly.

ANGIE
Andrew, if you touch me, you'll never touch me again.

ANDREW
I know. I know.

*Reluctantly, ANDREW takes ANGIE's arm. She jerks it away
and grabs his ring finger, forcing it back. ANDREW crumples
in pain. She holds it.*

ANDREW
Honey, that hurts. Sweetie, the pain—blinding.

ANGIE
Your mother taught me this.

*BIRGIT picks up the dropped handcuffs and cuffs ANGIE to
ANDREW. Surprised, ANGIE lets ANDREW go.*

BIRGIT

Must I do everything myself?

ANGIE

Damn it. What happened to civil disobedience? Freedom of speech? All that sort of stuff. This is Native land. I am Native. I have a Native opinion, goddammit!

BIRGIT

Nobody cares.

REINHART

Birgit, don't you think this is a little …

BIRGIT

One week 'til opening, Reinhart. We have little options. Take her away, Mr. Kakina.

ANDREW

Something deep inside tells mē I'm going to regret this far more than you are.

ANGIE

This is not a good beginning for our marriage, Andrew. You think I'm mad at you now … I am going to call your mother. I am going to have you declared dead. I am going to call all your ex-girlfriends and give them your credit card numbers.

ANDREW

Yeah. I know. I'm a dead man walking.

REINHART

I'm sorry, Ms White. Truly I am. I'll see what I can do.

ANGIE

I have only one thing to say to you, Mr. Reinholz. And Ms Heinze, *Ich bin Ojibway!*

REINHART

You left out the *ein*. It's pronounced *Ich bin ein Ojibway.*

ANGIE

Damn it!

BIRGIT

Take her away.

ANDREW

One question, sweetie. Squeeze-muffin. Um, are we still getting married?

They exit.

BIRGIT

Reinhart, have someone clean up this mess. I want everything perfect.

REINHART

Perfection is a difficult state to reach.

BIRGIT

Then put some effort into it. I will have perfection. Mark my words.

BIRGIT exits.

Scene Six

Back in DONALDA's office.

DONALDA

You did what!

ANDREW

Calm down. I'm only allowed one insane angry Ojibway woman a day. I'm past my quota.

DONALDA

How could you arrest her! You're supposed to be getting married next month!

ANDREW

What was I gonna do?! Say no? They would have brought somebody else in who might not have been so gentle. I gave her the best cell in the building. The toilet works and everything. This is all so screwed up. I know love is a battlefield but this is getting ridiculous. She's not talking to me.

DONALDA

I wouldn't either.

ANDREW

She's calling me horrible names.

DONALDA

How can she be not talking to you and calling you horrible names at the same time?

ANDREW

Oh, she can.

DONALDA

I am becoming less and less enchanted with these Germans.

ANDREW

I know. Who could have thought they could be so mean and efficient?

DONALDA

Any idea what you're gonna do?

ANDREW

None whatsoever.

DONALDA

When are visiting hours?

ANDREW

Whenever she stops throwing things. I'm wondering if maybe we sent out the invitations a little too early. What do ya think?

Suddenly, TRAILER enters.

TRAILER

Hey, hey, are they here? Have they arrived yet?

DONALDA

Has what arrived?

TRAILER

The buffalo. I've got one hundred and twenty-five coming in trailers today. One hundred and twenty-five big, beautiful fast-running buffalo. Now that's gonna make a damn decent stampede! And I've got them to work for scale!!! Next on my list, I need four Indians who are willing to fall off their horses during the buffalo hunt. Surprisingly, those are almost as hard to find as the buffalo. So far I've talked two of my brothers, Sting and Big Bopper, into it. Luckily, I'm the smart one of the family. Altogether I have one hundred and sixty three mighty animals. (*Pause.*) Hey Andrew ... can you ride a horse?

ANDREW

If I have to.

TRAILER

Can you ... say ... fall off a horse?

ANDREW

Only if I fall off the wagon first.

TRAILER

I can get you scale and a half.

ANDREW

Not for all sauerkraut in Germany. I think I liked the old Trailer better.

DONALDA

Me too. Trailer, I'm absolutely delighted that you got your buffalo. Really, I am. It's even cute how all their eyes and heads seem to follow you when you walk by them. But we've got a mini-crisis here, one that does not include buffalo of any kind.

TRAILER

Of course not. Nobody understands how difficult it is to put on a decent show. You don't understand the creative hell I'm in. Producers have feelings and worries too, you know. I'm practically dying putting this show together and nobody understands what I'm trying to achieve here. Fine. You deal with your mundane lives while I try to create art. Something that says a greater truth, a deeper statement about our people.

ANDREW

This would be *Dances With Wolves—The Musical?*

TRAILER

Exactly. Now if you'll excuse me. I have to shuffle off to the buffalo.

TRAILER exits.

ANDREW

Why is this place seeming more and more like Oz every day?

DONALDA

Andrew, I should tell you something. In view of what just happened to Angie, and Trailer's declining mental state, I've decided that I'm leaving the OjibwayWorld corporation.

ANDREW

But Pretty Gal, you started this whole thing. This is as much your child as it is the Germans'. You can't just walk out.

DONALDA

Sure I can. I'll just tell the Germans that walking out on your job is an ancient tribal tradition, right up there with sweatlodges and bingo. I'll blame it on the bad omens created by the migrating caribou interfering with my *North of Sixty* television reception.

ANDREW

Do you really think it's that bad?

DONALDA

(*looking out the window*) Oh look, they're putting the fake snow on Mt. Phil Fontaine. And they're testing the river that flows out of its peak. That's where tourists will white water kayak down into the Chief Dan George Gorge. Our ancestors would be so proud.

DONALDA exits. ANDREW sits there, pondering personal demons.

Scene Seven

The fair grounds. Silence. Then suddenly TRAILER comes running across the stage from stage left in a panic, screaming in total fear. Just as quickly, he disappears off stage right. Still screaming. Off in the distance, the bellowing and rustling of several large beasts can be heard.

Scene Eight

In BIRGIT's office.

BIRGIT

I have talked with the head office. They are most pleased with our efforts. Reinhart, we are so close. Please, share a glass of schnapps with me to celebrate.

REINHART

I do not like this.

BIRGIT

There are many things in this world not to like. Can you be more specific?

REINHART

I am hearing more and more voices of discontent. Many feel we've gone too far. I mean really, Birgit, the Crazy Horse Pony Ride? The Sitting Bull Steak House and Rotisserie? I ...

BIRGIT

Nonsense. Everything is on schedule. This has been my dream, Reinhart, for over twelve years. There is always some discontent to be expected. It will pass. This is a good thing we're doing. We're helping these people. Trust in that.

REINHART

I wish I had your faith.

BIRGIT

It's not faith. It's confidence. You should be confident. You designed a brilliant theme park. The most unique in the world. And it's about to come alive. It will delight and educate untold thousands and thousands of people. Be proud of that. Be confident in that.

REINHART

Somehow I cannot help but think it is not the vision we started out with so long ago. I have a bad feeling.

BIRGIT

In keeping with the spirit of the enterprise, might I suggest you take some aspirin. It comes from the bark of the willow tree, as discovered by Native people.

REINHART

There is no need to tell me the obvious.

BIRGIT

Since we are less than a week away from opening, I assume there must be a thousand little details that could use your attention. None of which are probably in my office.

REINHART

Very well, but mark my words, a dark omen is hovering over us all.

BIRGIT

Yes, yes. Dark omen.

At this point, DONALDA walks in the office, quickly and with a purpose. She puts a piece of paper down on BIRGIT's desk.

DONALDA

I quit. My letter of resignation. In triplicate—English, German and Ojibway. Gotta go. Bye.

Just as quickly, she exits.

BIRGIT

Your dark omen has a name.

REINHART

I told you so.

BIRGIT

Why would ...

DONALDA sticks her head back in the doorway.

DONALDA

One more thing. There may or may not be a long forgotten traditional burial ground located somewhere under the premises. Possibly underneath the Swampy Cree Water Park. Did I forget to mention that?

BIRGIT

But ... but ... you suggested that land! You helped us get all the permits. It was you who ...

DONALDA

Yeah well ... ooops. Sorry. And I hear there's a smallpox epidemic in the village. Anyway, just food for thought. Hope it's not a problem. Co-obmen.

DONALDA exits again, leaving behind some stunned Germans.

REINHART

This is not good.

BIRGIT

A burial ground! That could destroy us! Even if there isn't, the bad publicity alone ...

REINHART

What should we do?

BIRGIT

I don't know. I'll check the Aboriginal theme park emergency manual.

BIRGIT rummages through the book shelf behind her when TRAILER runs in, extremely excited and panicked.

TRAILER

Run! Run! For the love of God, run!

REINHART

Trailer, what is it?

TRAILER

Are you deaf! Don't just stand here, run! Flee! Hide! Panic! Just save yourselves!

BIRGIT

What's wrong? Calm down.

TRAILER

You don't understand! The buffalo ...

BIRGIT

Yes, about the buffalo, you are of course aware that technically they aren't really buffalos. That's a misnomer. They are actually an animal known as bison. Now what about the bison?

TRAILER

They're free, you crazy German! They're running amok!
Amok I tell you!

REINHART

I don't understand.

TRAILER

What is there to understand about crazed buffalo dammit!
It's a stampede, you fool! It's a herd of irate,
malcontented buffalo! Hide!

REINHART

But doesn't your show have a stampede written into it?

TRAILER

Not that kind of stampede, this is a real stampede. They're
out of control! I went to check them out, the new buffalo,
and I think the ones that had been here longer had been
… like … talking to them or something. In buffalo code.
They took an instant dislike to me. You could smell it in
the air. The moment I stepped into the pen area, they all
stared at me. They got them small eyes but their look can
be piercing. Then, it was the weirdest thing. They started
to all moo …

REINHART

Buffalo don't moo.

BIRGIT

Bison don't moo.

REINHART

Of course. You are correct.

BIRGIT

Thank you.

TRAILER

THOSE BIG HAIRY ANIMALS … or what ever you want to call
them, started gettin' agitated. Their calls started to ebb
and flow across the holding area, like they were
formulating a plan. Then suddenly, out of nowhere, one
of them attacked the fence. One by one they trampled the
fences until they were all free. All the time they were

staring at me. Watching me. Judging me. Then out of
nowhere, one of them gave a huge bellow and came
running for me. Before I knew it they were all running,
like a wall of hairy death and bad-smelling destruction,
cutting a path of devastation across the park. There's a
hundred and sixty-three bison loose in Otter Lake. A
hundred and sixty-three hoofed messengers of death!!!
Who do you call for something like that? Animal Control?!

BIRGIT
I don't believe this!

*Suddenly the sound of over a hundred buffalo/bison can be
heard off in the distance.*

REINHART
I believe it.

TRAILER
So I just came in to pick up my paycheque ...

The sound of metal and glass being destroyed can be heard.

REINHART
What's that?

TRAILER
I think that's my new Passat. It's now a doormat. I really
need my pay cheque now.

The sound of the buffalo diminishes.

BIRGIT
Where's Andrew Kakina? Park security is his responsibility.

REINHART
I don't know if that includes twenty-five hundred pounds
of charging animal flesh. I would find that rather
intimidating.

BIRGIT
It does. I made sure it was included in his contract.
Section 14, paragraph 12, subsection C—known as the
Charging Bison/Attacking Grizzly Clause. It's a standard rider.

TRAILER
Wow, you Germans do think of everything. Now, in
regards to my cheque ...

BIRGIT
Come, we must find the man.

The sound of more destruction can be heard, as well as the bellowing of the buffalo/bison. BIRGIT storms out the door, followed by REINHART and TRAILER.

Scene Nine

ANDREW's office. ANGIE is not in a good mood. She is throwing the darts from Scene One at ANDREW. He is ducking them.

ANDREW

Sweetie, I can tell you're upset. Your aim is off.

ANGIE

You realize they're turning us against each other. That's their big master plan.

ANDREW

They are not turning us against each other and there is no master plan. Have you always been this paranoid?

ANGIE

Pretty Gal believes me.

ANDREW

That's why she's called Pretty Gal, not Pretty Smart.

ANGIE

And Andrew, what about us? The wedding? Our lives?

ANDREW

I still love you very much.

ANGIE

You have a very funny way of showing it. Are you going to beat me with a rubber hose next?

ANDREW

Like that would stop you.

Suddenly, the phone rings. ANDREW answers it.

ANDREW

Andrew Kakina. (*Pause.*) Um, sure. (*Pause.*) Really? (*Pause.*) Okay, I'll look into it. Thanks.

ANDREW hangs up.

ANDREW

That was Stubby Johnson. Evidently the world's biggest and ugliest cow is eating his lilac bush.

ANGIE

Oh, I love that lilac bush.

Suddenly, DONALDA enters, excited.

DONALDA

Andrew?! What are you doing here? Shouldn't you be doing something?

ANDREW

Something is a rather broad term. Could you be more specific?

DONALDA

Angie, talk to him! Make him do something.

ANGIE

(*to ANDREW*) You're right. *Something* is a rather broad term.

ANDREW

Calm down, Donalda, and talk to me. What could possibly be that earth-shattering?

Then there is an earth-shattering rumbling that shakes the building. It is the sound of almost six hundred hooves approaching.

DONALDA

Haven't you heard! It's a flesh tsunami! They've already practically destroyed everything, including Stubby Johnson's lilac bush!

ANGIE

Wasn't that a nice bush?

DONALDA

The white one? I like Joanna Little's purple one better.

ANDREW

What are you talking about? And what was that noise?

BIRGIT, REINHART and TRAILER burst into the room, equally agitated.

REINHART

Good afternoon again, Pretty Gal.

BIRGIT

Never mind her. Mr. Kakina, why aren't you out there protecting our investment?

ANDREW

(*pointing at ANGIE*) I've taken her into custody and condemned myself to a living hell. What more do you want from me?

BIRGIT

I am not talking about her!

More rumbling is heard and the horrendous sounds of dozens of large beasts running amok in the town. ANGIE looks out the window.

ANGIE

Oh my God!!! There's a sea of what appears to be buffalo out there. Some sort off buffalo apocalypse.

TRAILER

They're called bison.

BIRGIT

The protection of this park is your responsibility, Mr. Kakina. I suggest you go out there and fulfill your contractual obligations.

ANDREW

You want me to stop a herd of rampaging buffalo?! With what?

BIRGIT

You have a gun I assume.

ANDREW

I have a revolver. The bullets will bounce off them.

BIRGIT

Your shocking lack of cultural knowledge is growing tiresome. Look deep within your ancestral roots and make a bow and arrow.

ANDREW

Out of what?! A coat rack and computer wire?

BIRGIT

I don't care. Mr. Kakina, I really must insist …

ANDREW

Insist all you want. I quit.

BIRGIT

You what!?

ANDREW

I quit. Or in German, *Ich bin hier weg …*

ANGIE

Now that's the Andrew I know and love. Though I'm a little hurt that it took a herd of crazy bison to make you quit, and not my pleadings.

ANDREW

You I can outrun.

BIRGIT

This cannot be possible. I will not allow it. This is my dream. Twelve years of my life. You—all of you cannot quit. I won't allow it. You are all fired. I will hire new people. OjibwayWorld will open.

> *More destruction can be heard outside. Especially one loud crash.*

REINHART

What was that?

DONALDA

(*looking out the window*) I think the laser beam dreamcatcher just fell on Trailer's trailer.

TRAILER

My trailer. My architecturally identical version of Graceland! Why!?

REINHART

I think it is over, Birgit. It was not meant to be.

> *BIRGIT is quiet for a moment.*

BIRGIT

I never liked buffalo meat. Fine. So be it. I am done with this place and with you. I will take the insurance money and move to Plan M, M & M.

DONALDA

Plan M, M & M?

BIRGIT

The Mohawk Mini-golf and Marineworld. I'm sure they will be more receptive. I tried to bring civilization and prosperity to this community, but perhaps I was ahead of my time. You weren't ready for OjibwayWorld. Fine. I shall leave you as I found you.

Come Reinhart.

BIRGIT moves to leave but REINHART doesn't move.

BIRGIT

Reinhart ...?

REINHART

I think I am not so quick to abandon this community. I think perhaps there is still something to be done here.

ANGIE

We're not going to start this all over again, are we?

REINHART

No, something smaller. More respectful. We've already got the substructure built and everything in place. I'm talking about something less garish. More grass roots. What do you think, Pretty Gal?

ANGIE

(*whispering to ANDREW*) I think he likes her.

BIRGIT

Stay here amongst the Anishnaabe if you must—

ANGIE

Finally, she gets the name right.

BIRGIT

Fine, I will create paradise all by myself. *Auf Wiedersehen.*

TRAILER/ANGIE/ANDREW/DONALDA

Sayonara, ciao bella, Au revoir, gracias, Hasta la vista, etc.

BIRGIT exits.

TRAILER

No dinner?

DONALDA

Count your blessings.

TRAILER

So, it's over. *No Dances With Wolves—the Musical?!*

REINHART

I'm sorry. No.

TRAILER

No Cirque du Billy Jack?

DONALDA

Sorry, Trailer.

TRAILER

But I promised my little brother a job! Ringo's gonna kill me. I should have stayed in my trailer.

DONALDA looks out the window.

DONALDA

Holy mackerel, it's going to take forever to clean up that mess. I'm not looking forward to filling out all the accident claim forms, damage caused by an act of buffalo.

REINHART/TRAILER

Bison.

ANDREW

Angie, what about us? Are we still going to get married?

ANGIE

I don't know. What's in it for me?

ANDREW

My undying love and gratitude.

ANGIE

What else you got?

ANDREW

I would marry you right now if I could.

ANGIE

Hey buddy, not all chicks who just get out of jail are horny and desperate.

ANDREW

Technically, you weren't in jail.

ANGIE

Arguing with me is not a way to get into my good books. Well, do you got any flowers?

ANDREW

Flowers? Buffalo ate them all.

ANGIE

Candy?

REINHART

I still have my Swiss chocolate.

ANDREW grabs it from REINHART.

ANDREW

For you, my sweet.

ANGIE

I don't know. Pretty Gal, what do you think?

DONALDA

Well, you realize that he's now unemployed—You'll have to support him.

ANGIE

I didn't think of that. Andrew, do something to impress me. Win me over. Prove your love.

ANDREW

I could write you a love poem.

ANGIE

I've read your poetry. Try again.

ANDREW

Okay. (*Takes a deep breath.*) Next April. Like you've always wanted. We'll fly to Boston and—run the marathon.

ANGIE

We will?! You will, with me?

ANDREW

I will. With you.

ANGIE

You'll train with me and everything?

ANDREW

Twenty-six long miles. Yeah, I'll train with you.

ANGIE
 And you'll love it?!

ANDREW
 And I will love it.

DONALDA
 Andrew, I thought you hated jogging.

ANDREW
 But I will love it.

ANGIE
 Pretty Gal, in retrospect, pickings are kind of lean around
 here. And I'd hate to have to retrain anybody. Fine, I
 think we've reached a deal, young man. You said you'd
 marry me right now. Let's be quick like a bunny about this
 before you change your mind. Hopefully a migrating herd
 of moose won't trash the reception.

REINHART
 Moose do not herd.

ANDREW
 But we don't have a minister or anything like that.

REINHART
 If I may. Several years ago I lived with the Lakota in South
 Dakota for several months, and was made an honorary
 Chief. While the position itself was honorary, I do believe
 I am entitled to perform traditional marriages. If you are
 interested.

ANGIE
 Damn Germans ... but what the hell. What do you say,
 Andrew? Feeling spontaneous? Down by the river. It's so
 beautiful there.

DONALDA
 Trailer and I can witness.

TRAILER
 If you want, for the wedding, I have a sixteen-piece
 orchestra that's currently out of a job.

ANGIE

But ... we don't have any rings. We need rings of some sort, don't we?

ANDREW

What happened to the ring I gave you last year?

ANGIE

I left it in the glove compartment of your security car.

ANDREW

I'll go get it then.

DONALDA

Ah, Andrew, when we came in here, we kinda noticed your car sort of, kinda, got in the way of the stampede. You'll need either a crowbar or a spatula.

ANGIE

Is there anything else we can use for a ring?

ANDREW

Ring—ring—

ANDREW picks up the discarded handcuffs.

ANDREW

How about these? I was going to save them for the honeymoon but, since we've already broken them out today ...

DONALDA

As somebody who used to be married, I think they're wonderfully symbolic.

ANGIE

Not exactly the traditional wedding I was hoping for but I can't think of anybody I would rather be handcuffed to.

REINHART

Then we're set. Shall we go then, to the river? Are you going to join us, Pretty Gal?

ANGIE

(*to ANDREW*) Told you.

DONALDA

You go ahead. Start without us.

REINHART, ANDREW and ANGIE exit.

DONALDA

Trailer, are you coming?

TRAILER

Everything has happened so quickly ... no musical—I worked so hard on it—my trailer—and the buffalo might still be out there. I'm telling you, I think they still have issues with me.

DONALDA

Cook for them and I'm sure they'll leave you alone.

She looks out the window.

DONALDA

Looks safe to me. Come on, you can be my date.

TRAILER

Your date? I can? Me? Uh, okay then. Yeah, them animals are probably halfway to the next county by now. Let's go to a wedding. Uh hey, Pretty Gal, my place is toast and I sorta need a place to stay, at least 'til I get my feet back on the ground.

DONALDA

A place to stay—? I don't know, Trailer.

TRAILER

I'll make dinner.

Arm in arm, they exit the building. All is silent for a second then a buffalo head or perhaps several heads can be seen peeking in a large window. They scan the room, look at each other and nod. They move towards the door that TRAILER exited, indicating they are following him.

Lights go down.

END OF PLAY.